Those Blessed

Leaders

Those Blessed Leaders

The Relevance of the Beatitudes to the Way We Lead

Peter Shaw

REGENT COLLEGE PUBLISHING
Vancouver, British Columbia

Dedicated to the students from around the globe studying for the MA in Leadership, Theology and Society at Regent College, Vancouver. May the integration of their studies and dialogue equip them to bring wise perspectives in demanding contexts.

Regent College Publishing
5800 University Boulevard
Vancouver, BC V6T 2E4 Canada

Regent College Publishing is an imprint of the Regent Bookstore (RegentBookstore.com). Views expressed in works published by Regent College Publishing are those of the author and do not necessarily represent the official position of Regent College (Regent-College.edu).

ISBN: 978-1-57383-596-1

Contents

Foreword

Set out in Matthew's Gospel with that familiar, proverb-like structure, the Beatitudes are not a code of behaviour, though the behaviour of those who take the Beatitudes to heart is bound to be affected, so much as a statement of those qualities of character that will bring to a life the greatest sense of fulfilment and purpose; and by individuals living such lives are others most effectively inspired and productively led. "Blessedness is about wholeness, fulfilment, and joy, and not just happiness" (chap. 3).

St. Paul wrote about the coherent whole being made from diverse parts, drawing on the necessary and unique contribution of a variety of gifts (1 Cor. 12). Personal ambition is most healthy when borne out of a belief, following humble reflection, that our God-given gifts and accumulated experience may suit us to leading others. It is a "cathartic starting point" to recognise our own vulnerability and inadequacy (chap. 4); to lead without losing that sense of humility takes courage, more so than leading to serve ego, and the humble leader will be the one to follow!

In this elegant reflection, Peter Shaw develops these ideas, seeing the Beatitudes and their apparently counter-intuitive, or at all events counter-cultural, messages as a blueprint for an attitude of mind and heart out of which calmness, and compassionately rational responsiveness, will grow inside and radiate out to others. That way inspiring leaders and leadership can develop, effective leaders leading others to be effective, where those who lead find they can "sit lightly with power … recognising how to use influence and authority well" (chap. 6).

The Beatitudes appear as the opening of the Sermon on the Mount, the most sustained single account of the teaching offered by Jesus during his life and, Christians believe, his core message to his followers. But you do not need to be a follower of Jesus, or have any religious faith, to be inspired by them. Here, after some general thoughts, each Beatitude is considered in turn, unpacked, its saltiness savoured and illustrated, before the reader is left with some questions to challenge and encourage them in their own leadership role or roles.

Peter Shaw has spent much of a second career, after a distinguished first career in the Civil Service including three Director General posts with significant leadership responsibilities of his own, as a leadership scholar, consultant and coach. I have known him for twenty years or so as we are members together of the Anglican congregation Peter serves as lay reader (licensed lay minister), and in recent years particularly I have benefitted from his wisdom, encouragement and experience as I sought appointment to the High Court Bench and embarked on a second career of my own as one of Her Majesty's senior judiciary. This monologue written during the dark days of the Covid-19 pandemic is full of Peter's insightful warmth and balanced, thoughtful guidance.

As Peter finds, the Beatitudes "provide an antidote to self-aggrandisement" while they also "prompt us to be bold and courageous" (chap. 12). Amen to that, and may they, and the reflections on them in this book, improve how you lead, in whatever setting that may be and whoever it may be you find yourself leading.

Sir Andrew Baker
Judge of the High Court, Queen's Bench Division and
the Admiralty Judge
Royal Courts of Justice, London

The Text of the Beatitudes

Now when Jesus saw the crowds, he went up on a mountainside and sat down. His disciples came to him, and he began to teach them. He said:

> Blessed are the poor in spirit,
>   for theirs is the kingdom of heaven.
> Blessed are those who mourn,
>   for they will be comforted.
> Blessed are the meek,
>   for they will inherit the earth.
> Blessed are those who hunger and thirst for
>   righteousness,
>   for they will be filled.
> Blessed are the merciful,
>   for they will be shown mercy.
> Blessed are the pure in heart,
>   for they will see God.
> Blessed are the peacemakers,

for they will be called children of God.
Blessed are those who are persecuted because of
righteousness,
for theirs is the Kingdom of Heaven.

Blessed are you when people insult you, persecute you and falsely say all kinds of evil against you because of me. Rejoice and be glad because great is your reward in heaven for in the same way they persecuted the prophets who were before you. (Matt. 5:1-11 TNIV)

I

Introduction

'The Beatitudes' are teachings of Jesus that set out a profound set of truths relevant for all those in leadership responsibilities irrespective of whether or not they bring a perspective drawn from a faith understanding. The Beatitudes challenge leadership norms for leaders and will always have a special place in the understanding of those who bring an explicitly Christian perspective as they encapsulate the Judeo-Christian heritage. A leader shaped by their Hindu, Jewish, Sikh, Muslim, Buddhist or Humanist perspective will often be bringing similar approaches based on their understanding about living responsibly with their fellow citizens.

To some the Beatitudes seem counter-intuitive as they can be read as implying weak, subservient and unrealistic characteristics which seem inappropriate attributes when leading in a fast-moving and hostile environment.

My belief is that the Beatitudes provide a valuable set of challenging touchstones for any leader in any context or culture, and are valuable for reflection about what leading well means at a time of major uncertainty. They both name reality and recognise that we can change the reality around us by our interventions.

Bombastic, opinionated leadership has been found inadequate whether in politics, business or sport. On the other hand, compliant leadership has often led to apathy and a loss of energy and drive. The Beatitudes provide a routeway between these two extremes.

The Beatitudes provide a call to both thoughtfulness and decisive action. They call for a mindset that removes clutter and brings a desire for clarity, compassion, gentleness, doing the right thing, mercy, purity, peace-making and a recognition of persecution. The Beatitudes shake who we are at our core, and face us into addressing our values, and our actions. They can unsettle us and stretch us. They shape our character as we tackle demanding leadership challenges in uncertain and potentially painful times.

The Beatitudes, seen as touchstones for reflection, provide insights about the way we might think and act in a range of different situations. If they are viewed purely as a precise ethical code that we must follow, we are likely to 'fall at the first hurdle' with their becoming as irrelevant as New Year resolutions. But the Beatitudes can help build our approach in different situations and enable us to reframe how we respond to the myriad of pressures we are addressing as leaders.

The Beatitudes provide a route to shaping our character and mindset in the way we lead, with us becoming increasingly authentic and humane in the way we experience the leadership of others and are experienced by those we lead. They provide a valuable perspective on the realities of leading well, and help us shape our authentic leadership character and voice going forward.

In this short book I refer briefly to the context for the Beatitudes as the introduction to the Sermon on the Mount. From that grounding we then explore briefly the relevance of the Beatitudes as a lens through which we can view leadership pressures and opportunities whatever our world view and spiritual context. We then look at each Beatitude in turn exploring how they might be relevant for leaders. Each chapter includes illustrative, hypothetical examples and some points for reflection.

My hope is that some phases from the Beatitudes will ring true for you as you address your leadership challenges in whatever sphere or culture you are in. I invite you to embrace the wisdom that is embodied in the Beatitudes and see your leadership challenges through the lens of the Beatitudes.

2

The Context of
the Beatitudes

The impressive book *Speeches That Have Changed the World* published by Quercus reproduces speeches that have had a profound influence. Included among many others are speeches by Oliver Cromwell, George Washington, Abraham Lincoln, Mahatma Ghandi, Winston Churchill, John Kennedy, Martin Luther King, Nelson Mandela, Mikhail Gorbachev, Elie Wiesel and Barack Obama.

The first speech in the book is the 'speech' by Jesus that we call the Beatitudes. The book describes the Sermon on the Mount, of which the Beatitudes are the introduction, as the essence of Christian teaching which has informed principles about how human beings should treat one another. The book draws attention to the influence of the Beatitudes well beyond Christian followers as the Beatitudes reinforced in people's minds Jesus as a moral reformer, political revolutionary, Palestinian peasant, or charismatic rabbi. The book suggests that to Christians he is all of these things, alongside their belief that Jesus had a unique relationship with God, evidenced through his birth, death and resurrection, thereby bringing salvation and hope to subsequent generations.

Jesus was a carpenter, teacher, brother, son and friend. He was sometimes a reluctant leader who Christians believe offered the way for human beings to be reconciled with God the creator and sustainer of life through his death and resurrection.

It is helpful to see the Beatitudes in their historical context. At that time there was overly heavy-handed leadership, social unrest, class division, poverty and highly infectious diseases. There are many echoes of these issues today. The thrust of the Beatitudes overturned the way leadership was experienced and spoke straight into the issues of the day.

The Sermon on the Mount which runs through chapters, 5, 6 and 7 of Matthew's Gospel sets out the main themes of Jesus' proclamations and teaching. The New Testament scholar Tom Wright, in his commentary on Matthew's Gospel, expresses caution about the perspective that the Sermon on the Mount is just wonderful teaching with the world being a better place if the teaching is followed. He suggests that if we just think of Jesus sitting there telling people how to behave properly, we miss what was really going on. He noted that these 'blessings', the 'wonderful news' that he is announcing, are not saying, 'try hard to live like this'. They are saying that people who live like this are in good shape. They should be happy and celebrate.

Tom Wright talks of the list of 'blessings' or 'wonderful news' as part of Jesus invitation initiating a new era. He describes Jesus as 'offering wonderful news for the humble, the poor, the mourners, the peace-makers', and describes the Beatitudes as part of God announcing a new covenant—a new lasting promise with his followers. Tom Wright places the Beatitudes as a continuation of themes from the Old Testament. He writes:

> In Deuteronomy, the people came through the wilderness and arrived at the border of a promised land, and God gave them a solemn covenant. He listed the blessings and the curses that would come upon them if they were obedient or disobedient (chapter 28). Now Matthew has shown us Jesus coming out of Egypt (chapter 2) through the water and the wilderness (chapters 3 and 4) and into the land of promise (chapter 4). Here, now, is his new covenant.

Tom Wright describes the Beatitudes as: 'A summons to live in the present in a way that will make sense in God's promised future; because that future has arrived in the present in Jesus of Nazareth. It may seem upside-down, but we are called to believe, with great daring, that it is in fact the right way up. Try it and see' (*Matthew for Everyone* [London: SPCK, 2012]).

The New Testament scholar Michael Green described the Sermon on the Mount as the supreme jewel in Jesus' teaching. The Beatitudes come like 'a bolt out of the blue' for any who think of religion as a sad and miserable affair. Michael Green suggests that there can be life where there is profound joy, a joy that no person and no circumstance can take away. He suggests that it is a blessedness for now and is not reserved for some nebulous future.

The Beatitudes provide a lens through which to view life both in terms of aspiration and in terms of the acceptance of the here and now. The individual who is mourning or experiencing persecution will be interlinking past experiences that encourage them, and future hopes that sustain them, alongside seeking to find some moments of release and even joy in the here and now.

Many of the Beatitudes feel counter-intuitive. How can the person who is mourning be joyful or feel fulfilled? And yet most of us, when we are mourning will often remember with special poignancy moments of joy with those no longer with us. It might feel counter-intuitive that being meek or gentle in our approach will influence an apparently blinkered leader. But a word said in kindness at an appropriate time or a question raised thoughtfully can shift thinking at key moments.

The Beatitudes are relevant individually as prompts in particular circumstances, but viewed together they provide complementary perspectives on human experience. The person who is mourning may also feel persecuted. But as they begin to have capacity to show mercy to others and become peace-makers, they move from recipients of the goodness of others into being hungry to bring hope for others.

It is pertinent that Matthew in his Gospel immediately follows the Beatitudes with the call of Jesus to his hearers to be the salt of the earth and the light of the world. Salt is a hidden influence that permeates whatever it touches and gives it flavour while preserving goodness. Light shows a way forward as well as identifying what has been hidden away or lost.

The leader who is influenced or shaped by the Beatitudes is sometimes bringing a hidden influence adding flavour and preserving the good. Sometimes applying the Beatitudes means shining a light on issues that need to be exposed or identifying future steps that might be taken. It often means shining a light on our inner landscapes and identifying issues that need to be exposed and future steps that can be taken.

3

What Does Being Blessed Mean?

Jesus lived at a critical moment in history which Jonathan Pennington describes as a 'track that runs both ways: coming from the past into the Sermon on the Mount and running through the Sermon to an understanding of what is human flourishing' (*The Sermon on the Mount and Human Flourishing* [Grand Rapids: Baker, 2018]). He sums up these two elements of human flourishing in two Greek words: *makarios* and *teleios*. The concept of *makarios* is about happiness or joyfulness. *Teleios* is about wholeness and fulfilment. Blessedness is about wholeness, fulfilment, and joy, and not just about happiness.

The Psalms talk of a range of circumstances in which an individual might be blessed or flourish. In Proverbs those who flourish are those who find wisdom and live wisely. The focus in the Sermon on the Mount on holiness and righteousness is central to the thrust of the Beatitudes in prompting a way of thinking that enables people to flourish and be fulfilled whatever is going on around them and whatever hard times they are going through.

Various translators have substituted the word 'happy', for the word 'blessed' while recognising that this word does not encapsulate all that is contained within the concept of blessed. No one word can fully encapsulate the significance of the word 'blessed' at the start of each beatitude. Perhaps it is a mix of being fulfilled and allowing oneself to flourish in whatever situation you find yourself in. There is a sense in which being blessed in any situation is to be at peace with yourself in that context and able to live with the pain or ambiguities that you are being subjected to. Happiness is fleeting. Blessedness can be an inner sense of calm and peacefulness.

Much has been written about what does it mean to be authentic as a leader. Being authentic does not mean acting randomly by whim, nor does it mean purely following personal preferences and inclinations. Being authentic involves reading a situation as it is and bringing an approach that is sensitive to the context and draws on your values and experience in a way that helps to provide or nudge a way forward. It is about being part of the drama and not a bystander.

The Beatitudes were at the heart of the messages that Jesus was consistently giving his disciples. He was encouraging them to develop a frame of thinking that allowed them to see reality and pain in the world around them and bring an uncluttered, open and realistic approach in their minds and hearts which enabled them to have a profound influence on both individuals and the wider society and culture.

In a similar way the Beatitudes provide an approach which may seem counter-cultural but if embraced can have a profound effect in shaping and nudging the way organisations, communities and cultures respond to external shocks and steer their forward direction.

4

Blessed Are the
Poor in Spirit

The first Beatitude is, 'Blessed are the poor in spirit, for theirs is the Kingdom of Heaven'.

The word 'poor' in Hebrew means to be bound down, afflicted, to be depressed, downcast, to be poor, and needy, to be humble or oppressed. The Greek word behind the word 'poor' means destitute. It denotes the destitution that causes the poor to seek help from others. In the Psalms the word 'poor' does not exclusively refer to the destitute. Psalm 70 refers to the 'poor and needy'. Psalm 69 refers to the 'poor and sorrowful'.

The Old Testament prophet Isaiah talks of being 'poor and of contrite spirit'. In Judaism in the last two centuries before Christ the term 'poor' was practically a synonym for saintly or pious behaviour. 'Rich' tended to mean worldly and irreligious, and 'poor' the opposite. There can be a strong sense of being impoverished in spirit, even when being rich with material goods.

The Gospel writer, Luke, in his list of Beatitudes refers to, 'blessed are the poor'. Matthew uses the phrase 'poor in spirit', which various commentators have suggested is because Matthew is wanting to speak to the rich and poor alike. This Beatitude is more concerned with individual emptiness than with wealth or poverty.

The Gospel writer, John, recounts the story of Nicodemus who was a rich man, a scholar of weight and reputation and a member of the Sanhedrin, meeting Jesus at night and recognising there was a poverty within himself. The result of the encounter for Nicodemus was both a new understanding of the significance of the teaching of Jesus and a deeper self-awareness. He discovered a blessedness that he had not known before and in that sense was born again. He embraced a renewed understanding with a new insight overcoming the darkness within.

This Beatitude is the foundation for the rest of the Beatitudes and the Sermon on the Mount. It is the antithesis of seeking high performance because its focus in not on attainment. The poor in spirit are aware that they cannot ultimately protect themselves, and neither money, nor influence, nor power can save them from suffering and death. Poverty of spirit is the starting point for embracing the reality of life. It is counter-intuitive to embrace poverty of spirit as a quality, but it is a cathartic starting point to recognising our vulnerability and inadequacy. Being honest about our poverty of spirit frees us from pretence and from the fear of not being able to live up to other people's expectations. The recognition that we are poor in spirit gives us a clear understanding of our flaws and inadequacies. It helps us face up to our own pride which is the most pervasive and subtle self-defence mechanism. It is perhaps because pride is so engrained in human nature that this Beatitude comes first.

Recognising that we are poor in spirit helps us review our approaches and actions to see how our pride, fears or failures have led us to do things that hurt bothers. A poverty of spirit can lead us to a sense of remorse, which then enables us to mourn over our actions and then to move through the stages in our journey through the Beatitudes to becoming more merciful, purer in heart and bringing peace. Perhaps a recognition of being poor in spirit is our starting point for the next phase of our leadership journey?

Theologians often refer to the concept of kenosis which was Jesus emptying himself through his birth as a baby when he took on the weaknesses and vulnerabilities of humanity, and then his acceptance of death on the cross. In his incarnation as a human being Jesus brought the presence of God into the world in radically different way. He brought the self-emptying invitation that 'whoever loses his life for my sake will find it'. Perhaps at the root of being poor in spirit is the emptying of deep-seated ambitions or preferences that have distorted our view of people and the opportunities around us.

Perhaps Jesus, when he refers to the poor in spirit, is speaking to those who realise they are truly needy, and have embraced and accepted their weaknesses rather than fighting against them. Paul Tillich referred to, 'the courage to accept acceptance'. It takes an inverted, counter-intuitive kind of strength to accept our weaknesses and our poverty of spirit.

The poor in spirit might discover that progressively they have been set free from the prison cell of pride and expectation. Jesus told a story about the demeanour of a publican and a pharisee as they approached the Temple. Jesus compared the honest expression of poverty of spirit in the approach of the publican, with the fullness of external excellence of the pharisee. It was the humble publican and not the pharisee who was beginning to experience the Kingdom of Heaven.

The recognition that we are poor in spirit enables us to look beyond outside appearances and our vulnerabilities meaning that we are less likely to be taken in by our own pride or reputation, or taken in by the apparent authority and reputation of others. We look beyond outside appearances in both ourselves and others and are not overawed by rhetoric that blinds or obfuscates.

Looking at the world around us through the lens of this Beatitude encourages us to link together physical, emotional, mental and spiritual poverty. We see emptiness as a starting point for new understanding. As we move into new spheres, we admit our vulnerability and are open to learn from those we engage with, whether they be rich or poor, expressive or sorrowful, assertive or contrite.

We are open to our assumptions being shifted in the light of experience. We seek to bring the courage to accept people as they are and enable them to become better versions of themselves. We understand our vulnerabilities and have learnt how to interpret and temper those vulnerabilities. This Beatitude prompts us, when we enter into a new leadership role, to empty yourselves of preconceived notions or prejudices. We can allow ourselves and others to start with a blank sheet of paper, listening carefully and weighing up the evidence so that fixed notions or baggage does not get in the way of thoughtful decision-making.

We may well have been driven by ambitions and have seen a pathway ahead. We have achieved successive qualifications or applied for roles that build on what we have done before. A sense of ambition has pushed us forward with a drive based on the best of reasons about making a difference in the spheres in which we are engaged.

But sometimes there are moments to empty ourselves of our ambitions. They might have blinkered us towards a particular version of success. We might realise that these ambitions are a contrary to what is most important for other members of our family. We need the courage to start again, regroup and assess how our gifts can be used in different ways to powerful effect.

Sometimes we need to pay attention to our inner poverty, owning our own powerless and failures. We need to face into and work through our own limitations. It is out of our self-reflection and vulnerabilities that our creativity and hopefulness for the future can grow. As we embrace our own brokenness and limitations with grace, we can offer the same grace and generosity of spirit to others. As we accept our own limitations we are the more able to help others to accept and work through their own limitations.

We keep coming back to the importance of discerning a deeper reality. We can be stuck in feeling the pain of the here and now. Looking ahead with an openness to people and situations which we had previously dismissed can bring new insights about ourselves and potential opportunities before us.

Sometimes we are thrown into situations when pre-conceptions are thrown out of the window. The Covid pandemic led to radical new thinking about balancing work and home life. It highlighted inequalities and forced a rethinking about what freedoms are most precious. It brought us back to recognising that we can take little for granted and need to build back up from a new securer foundation the values and beliefs that are most important to us. We have had to define what are the core realities that are most poignant for us.

Rasheed had always been treated as a golden boy. He had excelled through school and university and made the best possible use of the management development pro-gram at an investment bank. He was assertive, determined and at times self-opinionated. Sadly, he got into conflict with a senior leader in the bank and was asked to leave. He was devastated by this rejection and went into a spiral of feeling victimised and sorry for himself. Gradually he accepted that his over-confidence and aggressiveness had made him unpopular and liable to be exited.

Once Rasheed began to accept that his exit was par-tially his own fault it helped him to empty himself of being dominated by financial ambition and to be much more focused on learning about himself and how he could be influential in a wider variety of ways. Rasheed needed to become downcast to recognise his failings, and des-titute in order to recognise what he needed to build up again. There was a strength of character within him that, once it was set in the right direction, could be a powerful influence for good. Rasheed needed to keep reminding himself that a degree of sorrowfulness and an acceptance of vulnerability was necessary for him to keep the type of equilibrium which enabled him to be open to new insights and aware of how those around him were engaging with each other.

Rosemary was a manager in a care home for people with varying degrees of dementia. She sought to create an environment that was safe for people who were often downcast and feeling afflicted. There was a sorrowfulness in the home, but also times of laughter and kindness. When Rosemary was at risk of feeling sorry for herself, she looked at some of the residents knowing their personal stories and the sources of their current sorrow. She sought to create an atmosphere where care givers invited the residents to lean into their own sorrow and find there the strengths, resources, community and joys which helped to sustain them. She found it inspiring to observe those who might appear to have lost their inner spirit but who continued to have moments when they smiled.. She was continually encouraged by what she observed about the resilience of the human spirit and the way people found hope in their sorrows.

When Rosemary felt downcast and sometimes afflicted with bureaucracy she tried to smile at her own minor irritations. When she felt down, she sought to look through the lens of those in the home who had lost much of their mental and emotional capabilities. She felt blessed that she could enable vulnerable people to be safe. She recognised that her own vulnerabilities were enabling her to empathize more with the residents.

For Reflection

- When you feel downcast, afflicted or emptied, what new insights does that give you about yourself and those around you?
- When do you need to have the courage to accept your circumstances are not likely to change?
- What enables you to see your own vulnerabilities as insights which help you understand the travails that other people are going through?
- What ambitions might you need to let go of in order to become more openminded to accepting new openings that perhaps carry less status or esteem?
- How might you embrace being poor in spirit and not see it as your inadequacy?

5

Blessed Are Those
Who Mourn

The full Beatitude is, 'Blessed are those who mourn, for they will be comforted'.

Grief is an inescapable factor in human life and can sometimes cast its shadow even long before a fateful event. The Beatitudes come from a world where children were not protected from the facts of life or from the facts of death. In the Bible's Old Testament writings there were a range of meanings attached to the world 'mourn'. Samuel mourned for Saul long before Saul was dead. Isaiah wrote about the gates of Jerusalem mourning the fall of Jerusalem.

The language of mourning is frequent in the Hebrew scriptures. There is a whole category of Psalms which are called lamentations of which Psalm 22 is the most poignant. In this Psalm the Psalmist talks about being forsaken and finding no rest. The Psalmist writes, 'My mouth is dried like a potsherd, and my tongue sticks to the roof of my mouth: you lay me in the dust of death. . . . All my bones are on display; people stare and gloat over me. They divide my clothes among them and cast lots for my garments, but you, Lord, do not be far from me. You are my strength; come quickly to help me'.

In ancient Israel there was a normal time limit for mourning. For example the Israelites grieved for their leader Moses in the plains of Moab for thirty days until the time of the weeping and mourning was over. The assumption was that life then moved on.

Isaiah talks of 'being called to proclaim freedom for the captives, release from darkness for the prisoners and comfort for all who mourn'. The book Ecclesiastes talks of wisdom coming with sorrow. The more knowledge the more grief. Ecclesiastes ends with a passage about a man going to his eternal home with mourners going about the streets with the sad refrain that, at the end, everything is meaningless.

The Prophets mourned the iniquities of Jerusalem long before they mourned its demise. The sense of mourning for personal and national errors is exemplified in the famous passage in Isaiah 53, 'He was despised and rejected by others, a man of suffering, and familiar with pain'. Luther translates the word 'mourn' with the phrase, 'sorrow-bearing': ie he bore our griefs and carried our sorrows.

Whenever Jesus spoke to crowds there would have been mourners who heard him: perhaps they were mourning the death of a family member or were bowed down with adversity of one kind or another. There would have been mourners because of sickness, and mourners looking back over their past recalling actions they regretted that they had done or had not done. Mourners listening to Jesus might have been lamenting a disastrous relationship. In the midst of their sorrows, a message of the Beatitudes is that blessedness (or happiness, joy, wholeness or fulfilment) is possible even in moments or situations dominated by mourning. In such painful circumstances authentic new life can be found that is uplifting even in pain.

We are all bound with mortality and are all mourners in some respects. We might have taught ourselves a way of handling our mourning, even smiling at what had been or might have been. This may be a lesson we need to keep relearning at each phase of life.

The New Testament for 'mourn' is *pentheo*, which means 'to grieve, lament or sorrow'. It is the kind of deep mourning that demonstrates emotional agony. Jesus specifies no specific objective for the mourning in this Beatitude. It could be grieving over the conditions of the poor and the disenfranchised. Standing on the Mount of Olives and looking over Jerusalem Jesus wept over its failings and the consequences of its sin. He grieved as though Jerusalem was being destroyed at that moment, rather than forty years into the future.

Mourning can come in different ways. It might be the loss of hope or an encounter with a truth that penetrates our defences and is a painful reminder of what might have been. Sometimes mourning can be triggered suddenly through a memory or a certain sound or sight. It can trigger melancholy about something that has long gone. Perhaps we have lost someone or something that was deeply precious to us. Mourning can be deep, dark, and disorienting. And no human being can escape mourning.

In one sense the Beatitudes invite us to face honestly into our own mourning. We might find after some reflection that mourning puts our experiences into a context that links the past, the present and the future. Mourning takes us deep into ourselves. It reminds us to make room for our emotions, for loss, for letting go, for the pain of others. With grief comes loss of control as the events we are experiencing are irreversible.

There need to be moments of lament to enable us to grieve and then to move on. When we spend time with our losses we can see how they have shaped us. We need to accept the silences that come with our losses and seek not to be overwhelmed by awkward or uncomfortable moments. We need ways of saying goodbye and thank you, even when we feel distraught inside.

Loss is an inescapable fact of human life. We mourn communities that we used to be part of. We might even mourn the loss of a team at work with whom we worked particularly closely. But from each loss there can be some experience or insight that carries us forward into the next phase of our lives. We cherish the memory of those who have influenced us in the past with some of their characteristics still living on within us.

We can sometimes mourn for what might have been and can become overwhelmed by a failure to take opportunities. Sometimes it is not easy to be released from the grip of what might have been and recognise that we can move through mourning into new beginnings.

We mourn in advance of sadnesses. As a team begins to lose members or its sharpness, there can be a growing realisation that the team is less effective and, therefore, will need to break up. It is then difficult to celebrate some on-going successes within the team if it feels increasingly clear that it is going to dissipate.

Grief can put life into perspective. It can be a blessing to be released from worry about someone who is in constant pain. I have worked with a number of people for whom a period of grief has been cathartic and fundamentally changed some of their life priorities. The mourning about not getting a particular role has released them from preoccupation about a particular status and enabled them to explore other avenues with fresh openness and energy.

There are times when mourning can become self-indulgent. Mourning about the loss of an opportunity can blur an openness to other opportunities. Mourning about what might have been can result in a lack of curiosity about what else might be possible.

Sorrow can be contagious or cathartic. A heavy burden of unremitting sorrow after a while can kill relationships. But sorrow that is lived through and articulated can lead to renewed purpose with a changed frame of reference and renewed set of aspirations. We integrate our losses into our lives going forward. As we keep past memories alive we use our past experiences to help us find the courage and strength to keep going. The vicarious carrying of sorrow for others for a season can enable us to cope in the moment and come through our mourning into a new place of understanding. There are moments when we all carry sorrows for others within our families and communities.

When an organisation needs to reduce the number of employees there can be a deep sorrow about the necessary departures and severances. The leader needs to enable those leaving to mourn the loss of their jobs, and those staying to mourn the break-up of the community. Enabling people to mourn and come through necessary mourning is an important quality in effective leadership.

Sometimes we might mourn the moving on of a good colleague or team member and are thoughtful about whether, if we had treated them differently, they might have stayed and not moved on. Reflecting in advance about whether we would mourn or celebrate someone's departure can provide useful data about our approach and engagement with them over the next period.

We have all been through grief in our personal lives. The stages of grief are just as pertinent in the work context as in the personal context. We are all bounded by mortality. We need to allow ourselves and others to mourn and then enable people to move on.

In 1995 I was the HR Director for the UK Government's Department for Education which was merged at two hours' notice with the Department for Employment. I held an evening party a few weeks later that was in effect a wake for staff of the Department for Education in which we collectively celebrated what the Department had done, mourned its demise and began to touch into the possible future. In my speech at the wake, I drew from Ecclesiastes referring to:

> A time to plant and a time to uproot,
> A time to tear down and a time to build,
> A time to weep and a time to laugh,
> A time to mourn and a time to dance.

The wake is referred to over twenty-five years' later when I meet people who were there as a cathartic and moving event where we mourned, celebrated and looked to the future at the same time.

Comments can trigger mourning which can catch us unaware. When we mourn for a team we used to be part of, or an opportunity we didn't take, how best do we recall the good things that did then transpire, even though they might not have been what we had previously sought or anticipated? When mourning is triggered it can lead to exploring our motivations and potential new insights and not just sad remembrances.

Aanya was very influenced by her Hindu tradition of marking thirty days following the death of a family member and then opening all the windows and letting the spirit of that person go back to God. Her faith had embedded within her the importance of mourning deliberately and thoughtfully, and then moving on and looking to the future.

Aanya had been very committed to the leadership team of which she was part. She was described as a key enabler for the team who understood where people were coming from. When two members of the team left, she encouraged the team to mourn the passing of a phase, while also encouraging them to let go of that belief that there was only one way in which the team could work effectively together.

Aanya drew insights from her faith perspective about mourning deliberately and then was explicit about moving on and looking to the future and not the past. Aanya was the catalyst for setting up the new team with its new members bonding effectively and looking to how they were going to engage well as a team going forward.

Andrew had been very influenced by what he believed to be the expectations of his Father. As his Father's health declined Andrew began to mourn the energetic person his Father used to be and recognised that it was now the son Andrew who was making decisions. By force of the new circumstances Andrew had to take the lead more within the family.

In the work context there was a parallel change for Andrew. He had stopped feeling he had to live up to the expectations of his successful Father. It began to be easier for Andrew to sit lightly to the expectations of others and to be more explicit about the role he needed to play in the organisation of which he was part.

For Reflection

- What helps us mourn well so that we celebrate and mark what has happened and can move into our own futures?
- How best do we sit with our own grief and work through a season of lament?
- What helps us put grief into proportion and bring a perspective that enables us to sit with grief and not be overwhelmed by it?
- When is it helpful to carry the sorrow of others and when do those sorrows need to be laid down?

- In what ways has mourning been a blessing in terms of being able to remember well and move on with hope and expectation?

6

Blessed Are the Meek

The full Beatitude is, 'Blessed are the meek for they will inherit the earth'.

This saying flows out of Hebrew thinking. The Psalmist talks of, 'the meek will inherit the land and enjoy peace and prosperity'. The word meekness frequently appears in Ecclesiasticus: for example, 'incline your ear to a poor man and answer him with decent words in meekness'. Jacob is described as someone of faithfulness and meekness.

Moses' reputation of meekness did not derive from timidity. He stood before Pharaoh unafraid and led an intransigent people with clarity and subtlety during forty years of pilgrimage. The prophet Isaiah speaks approvingly of those who are meek and of contrite spirit. The prophet Zechariah looks forward to the day when the Messiah comes both meek and riding on an ass.

Psalm 37 links meekness, patience and trust. Meekness is linked to commitment, with the meek advised to refrain from anger. The relevant section from Psalm 37 is as follows:

> Commit your way to the Lord; trust in him and he will do this: He will make your righteous rewards

shine like the dawn, your vindication like the noon-day sun.

Be still before the Lord and wait patiently for him; do not fret when people succeed in their ways, when they carry out their wicked schemes.

Refrain from anger and turn from wrath; do not fret – it leads only to evil. For those who are evil will be destroyed, but those who hope in the Lord will inherit the land.

A little while, and the wicked will be no more; though you look for them, they will not be found.

But the meek will inherit the land and enjoy peace and prosperity.

The Greek word *praus*, which translates as 'meek', can also be translated as gentle, considerate, humble and exercising self-control. Jesus brought those qualities in the way he built up his followers and engaged with the crowds. In his ministry of healing he brought gentleness, patience and considerateness. But he could also be scathing about the attitudes of the powerful and was a skilful debater in public. He turned over the tables of the money changers in the Temple when he felt that the Temple was being abused: he was capable of demonstrating righteous indignation. He discouraged resentment and impatience amongst his disciples. Jesus combined being gentle and considerate, alongside being clear and direct.

Meekness and gentleness are closely linked in a way that makes them interchangeable. Paul, when writing to the Philippians, encourages them, 'let your gentleness be known to all'. The Beatitude is encouraging a meekness that is a subtle blend of patience, gentleness and considerateness on the one hand, alongside a deliberate approach to enabling change to happen which is rarely angry and never malicious.

Meekness may feel counter-intuitive and moves in a different way from our instincts. In a difficult situation there might be the natural instinct of either 'fight or flight'. Meekness might mean finding a 'third way'. It is not about meeting force with force, nor is it about abject compliance. C. P. Sturgeon talked of, 'meekness involving contentment with a multiple desire to make use of their talents in a way that is not anxious, fretful, grieving or grasping'.

This Beatitude would not have seemed to Jesus as outrageous or paradoxical as it may seem to us. His hearers may have been far from meek themselves, but would have known what was meant and would have understood the reference to the meek not only inheriting heaven, but also inheriting the earth.

Meekness involves blending gentleness with decisiveness, patience with purposefulness, and compassion with clarity. Meekness involves sitting lightly with power, while recognising how to use influence and authority well. Meekness does not equate with timidity and servitude, but it does influence how points are made and legitimises gentleness and patience as part of the repertoire of a leader who wants to ensure clarity of purpose and change that is sustained.

Knowing that we are poor in spirit and that we mourn our inadequacies and failures can lead us to an honest and humble look at ourselves. This equips us to be understanding and be compassionate of others in their challenges, approaching them with gentleness, openness and meekness, not being overly judgemental and forceful. Fostering meekness helps us to bring our own humanity and experience into each situation we enter, with a focus on enabling others to thrive rather than demonstrating that our ideas are right. Key is being aware of the power we hold as a leader and then holding it lightly.

Meekness involves regularly seeking to find a new way of tackling issues that is sensitive to the concerns and preferences of others whilst not being subservient to whims, historic predilections or individual self-interest.

Meekness can open up the power of possibilities. The gentle and persistent question about what might be done differently can, over time, create an openness to ideas and erode the impact of dogmatism. Bringing meekness will not involve backing down at the first instance. It may well mean collecting further evidence and talking to a wider range of people so that with gentleness and fortitude an embryonic idea is turned into a coherent and apposite way forward.

Those who sit lightly with power often use it more effectively than those who see power as a right that justifies unbending assertiveness. The meek leader recognises they only hold authority for a season and that they are dependent on others to retain that authority and for its wise use. The meek leader is listening to the views of past clients and customers and is attuned to dialogues that are going on around them.

Meekness means controlling the natural impulse to show anger and is the opposite of being quick-tempered or vindictive. On the other hand, meekness may well involve direct challenge when power is being abused. Meekness is not about grasping power, but it can be about clarity and directness. Sometimes it does include showing discontent when there is injustice, but in a way that brings objectivity based on evidence rather than heightened emotions.

Sometimes a burning platform has to be described bluntly. Sometimes there needs to be a bonfire of previous perspectives. A problem needs to be exposed and addressed. This is a moment to speak and act clearly. This is not counter to bringing meekness. It means that there is respect for facts and realities, and a courtesy in the necessary directness.

The meek leader has an inner life as well as an external personal. In the inner life there can be careful reflection about the balance between patience and decisiveness, between gentleness and directness. Within the inner life there might be a secure acceptance of why they as an individual are in their current location and how they are going to handle uncertainty or anxiety within their own framework, rather than letting it have a deleterious effect on them and those around them. In the inner life there can be a gentle awareness and exploration of the issues we ourselves bring to situations, and of our strengths and limitations, of areas to be healed, and of hope and possibility of a path as yet unwalked. There can be an exploration of our inner landscape which takes us into new areas where courage and resilience are needed.

Joanne found her boss authoritarian. As a consequence, she felt timid and anxious in his presence, and was unwilling to challenge him. Joanne concluded that confronting her boss directly was not going to work, but she recognised that she needed to be persistent in putting together evidence that pointed to the need for a change of direction. Joanne was deliberate in choosing the questions she raised and the occasions when she felt she could put alternative approaches on the table in discussion with her boss. Her manager was intrigued by her gentle and persistent approach and began to recognise the quality of her observations.

Over time, Joanne allowed herself to become more assertive with her boss while her boss increasingly accepted the quality of what Joanne was saying. If her boss became edgy Joanne did not respond in kind: she recognised that her boss would calm down quite quickly if there was a natural break in the conversation. There was an inner resolve in Joanne which meant that she was going to use her own authentic approach in seeking to influence her boss in a way that was consistent with her values. She was not going to allow herself to be timid or overwhelmed.

Harry had built a reputation as someone who could always see the logic in a range of different points of view and would then suggest alternative ways forward which drew on the best ideas from different people. Harry was quietly authoritative based on a reputation that had developed over a number of months. Team members drew in Harry because he brought a wider perspective and asked questions that prompted different ways of addressing issues. There was a gentleness in Harry that his colleagues liked. But they also greatly respected his way of thinking which was able to join the dots and identify different ways of tackling an issue.

For Reflection

- In what respects do you see meekness as a helpful or unhelpful quality?
- Where does gentleness and patience fit into your approach to leading?
- When are you at risk of being over dogmatic and not allowing open, thoughtful questioning?
- How much do you nourish your inner life, allowing meekness to become a more rounded quality in yourself?
- When is meekness in others inspiring to you?
- Might you invite input from others about how they experience you and your leadership in terms of what sort of meekness you demonstrate?

7

Blessed Are Those Who Hunger and Thirst for Righteousness

The full Beatitude is, 'Blessed are those who hunger and thirst for righteousness, for they will be filled'.

Righteousness can appear to sum up a self-indulgent belief that you are right. The aura of self-righteousness sets a tone of dogmatism and a lack of listening and appreciation of others. To the Hebrew mind righteousness meant something much more positive. In the Hebrew Scriptures righteousness is often linked with justice and bringing right-relatedness with God, self and others.

When Amos, the Old Testament prophet, is critical of noisy, self-indulgent assemblies, he concludes, 'let justice roll on like a river, righteousness like an ever-falling stream'. For the Hebrew righteousness implied a quality of relationship with both God and those around them. Isaiah exhorts his hearers to 'stop doing wrong, learn to do right, seek justice and encourage the oppressed, defend the cause of the fatherless, plead the case of the widow'. Isaiah links righteousness and being noble.

In the New Testament righteousness is often associated with those who claimed to be supreme practitioners of it, namely the Pharisees in protecting the purity of the religious tradition. When Jesus was talking to the Pharisees he said, "I have not come to call the righteous but sinners". Elsewhere in the Sermon on the Mount, Jesus said, "I tell you that unless your righteousness passes that of the Pharisees and the teachers of the law, you will certainly not enter the kingdom of heaven.' In the Greek world the word 'righteous' describes someone possessing virtues like prudence, justice, temperance and fortitude.

This Beatitude would have resonated with the Hebrew focus on righteousness being about relationships that are building the common good, alongside the focus on virtues like prudence, justice, temperance and fortitude. Our understanding of the word 'righteous' is clouded by its association with the Pharisees which suggests a 'holier than thou' attitude alongside a critical spirit and rigidity of mind. In the New Testament the Pharisees are depicted as standing for strict obedience to the letter of the law as a means of achieving righteousness. For the early Christians righteousness flowed from living a faithful life embracing and embodying the new life and approach that Jesus brought.

The introductory phrase to the Beatitude about those who 'hunger and thirst' for righteousness is significant. This is not about a passing or fleeting desire, but something that runs deep in an individual's heart and mind and is constant and on-going. The Beatitude represents a deep longing. It echoes words from the prophet Hosea about God caring for people in the wilderness in a dry and dusty land.

This Beatitude starts with an expectation about a strength of intent to bring a distinctive way of interacting with others that seeks to bring justice and a clear focus on what is the right thing to do in different situations. C. P. Spurgeon talks of the Beatitude demonstrating an insatiable longing to make a significant difference in the spheres in which people live. It implies an earnest desire rather than fainthearted energy.

It is significant that this Beatitude about hungering and thirsting for righteousness immediately follows the Beatitude about meekness. Taken together they suggest the importance of clarity of intent and the determination to make a difference, alongside a sensitivity to be gentle and patient in our resolve.

As leaders we cannot afford to feel superior and behave like Pharisees following a legalistic interpretation of what is the right thing to do. Seeking righteousness will always involve a focus on justice and fairness. It will be deliberate in seeking to have a constructive effect on the worlds in which we operate.

Righteousness is about bringing an authentic belief in fairness that is willing to stand up to prejudice. It is inciting us to be bold in clarifying what is the right thing to do in any situation and then accepting the responsibility on our shoulders to challenge the unreasonable exercise of authority. It is also being willing to seek the truth, even if it is not the popular view, including looking at issues from multiple angles.

This Beatitude is relevant at many different levels. There is a cautiousness about those who are self-righteous and exercise their authority in damaging and indulgent ways. There is a strong link between righteousness and justice whereby there is a call to seek to build a more just society where there has been proper discussion about what is fairness and appropriate justice. An insatiable longing for justice has shaped and continues to shape the vocation of leaders in different spheres.

Creative righteousness is about bringing an open and innovative approach to thinking through how problems might be addressed in new ways where the results support and motivate a wider range of people. Someone's assertiveness may be right technically, but if they have failed to develop in others the hunger and thirst for a particular outcome, then belief in the righteousness of what they are seeking to do may be of little consequence. Righteousness is about the quality of relationships as much as the fairness of the intent.

As a participant in any organisation, we respect those with clarity of thinking but always need to be wary about those who always believe they are right, because of their status or because they feel superior to others. Just as Jesus stood up to the Pharisees, there are times when any leader needs to speak truth to power when authority is being misused, provided they do not themselves fall into the trap of believing that they are always right. Being authentic means being willing to say what you believe is right, but it also means listening carefully with openness to the perspectives of others.

Hungering for righteousness, for truth, for honest business practices, for doing things right needs to be both foundational and also daily practice. Our strategic plans, our employment practices, our financial activities should flow out of hungering to do the right things in an ethical way. At the heart of the search for righteousness is respecting the perspective of others whose world view is different to our own, while seeking to find a way forward that respects the evidence and enhances and does not undermine the lives of our fellow citizens.

Pat was sometimes teased by his colleagues by being called 'Pious Pat'. He wondered whether this was a negative comment or a mark of respect. He did not want to be seen as a negative influence. On the other hand, he would frequently refer to the agreed values for the organisation when it came to discussion about what might be the right next steps in addressing a particular issue.

Pat was careful not to seek to give any impression that his views were somehow better than others, but in a gentle and persistent way he saw it as his role to seek to ensure that discussion with colleagues was based on objective thinking about how individuals were affected by different choices. He did not want to dampen the enthusiasm of his colleagues but wanted to ensure their creativity was within a framework that would lead to fair, thought through outcomes.

Pat would gently smile and not show any irritation when he was referred to as Pious Pat, but he did take that comment as a reminder about the importance of ensuring quality, open and engaging relationships with all his colleagues which allowed him then to suggest approaches that his colleagues might initially not warm to. He was conscious that he needed to point out the truth in situations without being too easily dismissed as being over pious.

Chloe felt that a number of her colleagues had become complacent. They believed that the Social Work Department of which they were all a part was doing fine in the current circumstances. To the extent that they were limited in what they were able to do they regarded this as the result of decisions by politicians and the lack of resources. The social workers were doing a useful role which they felt was unappreciated and, therefore, they were not going to be particularly motivated to try new approaches.

Chloe felt that this self-righteous and indulgent perspective was draining the energy out of the team and unhelpful. It had become quite deep-rooted and difficult to shift. Chloe with some reluctance applied for the post of leading the team knowing that she had to deal with a group of people who were feeling quite self-righteous: but there was a hunger in her to seek to shift the perspective in the team because of the importance of the work they were doing in the local community. Chloe knew this would be a difficult path but, with some hesitation, she was committed to build relationships with her colleagues that would hopefully shift their attitude into a more constructive space.

For Reflection

- What is the risk that you can appear a touch self-righteous?
- How best do you handle those who always believe they are right?
- What for you is the link between righteousness and justice and how best do you build fairness and justice in the spheres in which you operate?
- What might creative righteousness mean for you in terms of adapting your approach?
- To what extent might an insatiable longing for justice grip the way you use the leadership opportunities available to you?
- In what areas of your life might you sense a self-righteousness or a lack of righteousness and what might help you shift that attitude into a more constructive place?

8

Blessed Are the Merciful

The full text of the saying is, 'Blessed are the merciful for they will be shown mercy'.

This Beatitude provides a lens through which we can view life and provides a clear nudge in a particular direction. It provides a touchstone about how best we make decisions and reminds us that others will often mirror our behaviours. The idea of mercy is a recurring theme in the Hebrew scriptures. In the Psalms alone it occurs 120 times translated variously as loving kindness, goodness or good deeds. In the Hebrew scriptures God's mercy is inseparable from the call to be merciful to others.

Showing mercy was a key theme in the teaching of Jesus. The parable about 'the Prodigal Son' could equally have been called, 'the Merciful Father'. Jesus quotes the words of the Prophet Hosea, 'I desire mercy and not sacrifice'. Mercy was close to the heart of Jesus. He never tired of talking about it and embodying mercy in his actions.

The same emphasis is embodied in the approach of Paul who was the biggest critic of the Christian faith and then became a strong advocate. He wrote to the young leader Timothy that Christ had shown mercy to him,

Paul, the worst of sinners, through demonstrating unlimited patience with him. Perhaps the most poignant of the prayers from Anglican liturgy is the prayer of humble access which sums up so much of the teaching from the scriptures. It includes the phrase, 'we do not come to this thy table trusting in our own righteousness but in thy manifold and great mercies'.

When we become aware of our poverty of spirit and are humbled by that reality, and then hunger for righteousness we become aware of how much we need mercy and forgiveness. When we forgive ourselves for own mistakes and seek forgiveness from those we have wronged or let down, we have greater capacity to show mercy to others.

Are mercy and justice compatible or contradictory? Jesus told the parable of the unforgiving servant. The master had mercy on the servant who begged for patience in paying off his debts. This servant then demanded payment from a fellow servant with no similar concession. The result was that the Master called back the servant whose debt he had let off and had him put in jail until he paid back all he owed. The punchline in Matthew's account of this story is about the importance of forgiving others from the heart. In this parable the master shows both mercy and justice. Mercy is shown to the servant who pleaded for patience, but when this servant does not himself exercise patience, the Master sends him to jail.

The positioning of this parable about the unforgiving master is so interesting as it is prefaced by the dialogue between Peter and Jesus about the need to forgive 'not seven times, but seventy-seven times.' The parable then ends with the Master sending the servant to jail and not appearing to forgive him for his apparent first offence. Jesus knew that Peter was finding it hard to forgive and so Jesus was emphasizing the importance of forgiving and not bearing a grudge. At the same time Jesus was reinforcing the need to hold mercy and justice in balance.

Is there ever a risk of showing too much mercy? There will be different perspectives on this. As a result of the call to be merciful many organisations have had a tendency to be too lenient in dealing with inappropriate behaviour when people have manipulated or abused others. There is a risk for leaders, especially in the voluntary sector, of being too forgiving and in seeking to show mercy and forgiveness to one person when ignoring the pain that that individual has been causing to others. There is a risk that we can focus on what it means to forgive and love one neighbour, when not showing fully practical love for the people the individual has been causing pain to.

Mercy never operates in a vacuum. When we show mercy to one person there are always consequential effects. We can never view in isolation our way of responding to one person. Others will be affected whatever we decide when balancing justice and mercy.

Sometimes decisions that look harsh are done for caring reasons. During the Covid-19 epidemic prison governors had to implement a policy of locking up prisoners for twenty-three hours a day to limit the risk of the spread of Covid-19. Was this confinement a caring thing to do? Yes, in protecting physical health, but it inevitably had negative consequences in terms of people's mental health. Prison governors had a difficult path to tread caring for prisoners in a way that limited their freedom. Locking them up for 23 hours a day was hardly merciful in one sense, but in another this policy of isolation was merciful in trying to limit the spread of a killer virus.

For some loving kindness equates with being merciful. Showing kindness draws on listening well, bringing a generosity of spirit and speaking truth when things need to be said in a supportive way. It is normally not kind or merciful to connive with someone's self-delusions, although there are exceptions to this including when someone is suffering from dementia. Being merciful might be walking alongside someone to help them face into harsh reality, allowing them to work towards a way forward.

In a fast moving world leaders need to be courageous and make decisions where there is limited available data. Alongside a focus on being courageous needs to be an acceptance that if people are to experiment and take risks there will be some things that don't work as hoped. Alongside being courageous needs to be an acceptance that mercy and forgiveness need to sit alongside encouraging boldness.

There are times when it is right to show mercy through solving someone else's problem. There are times when showing mercy is about enabling someone to take responsibility for their own next steps. Jesus was merciful towards the disciple Peter, after he had denied him three times, but expected Peter to take responsibility to learn from what had happened and lead the emerging church.

I was working with the CEO of a Christian Charity recently about what does showing mercy mean to anyone who failed to live up to the expected standards of behaviour in the organisation. She said that if the individual was contrite, she would forgive them, but if their behaviour would normally have led to dismissal, she would dismiss them. For the CEO showing too much mercy by reinstating someone whose behaviour was unacceptable was neither good for the individual nor the Charity.

In what ways might we be blessed if we are merciful? We have all been captured by emotions like frustration, regret and even anger caused by our reactions to what others have done. When we are merciful to others and to ourselves, we can be released from these emotions of frustration, regret or anger that can eat us up. When we are merciful and let go of these negative emotions, there can be a sense of liberation and release. As a burden is lifted, we can feel lightened and blessed.

When we are merciful to others there is a greater likelihood that others will be merciful to us. If we show we are listening to others there is more likelihood that they will listen to us. The natural inclination is that people will mirror each other's behaviour.

As we bring loving kindness into any group or community of which we are part, we can be contagious and help influence a culture that is more merciful, while being mindful that bringing generosity of openness can lead to the risk of being taken advantage of.

When we bring a sense of loving kindness to demanding work situations, we can be more influential than perhaps we realise. We may feel that kindness is brushed aside, but over time there can be an acceptance that respect and kindness for each other, in the busiest of situations, can enable more progress to be made than we had thought possible.

Examples of being merciful can be very poignant. My father-in-law was a doctor with the Allied Forces in the D-Day landings. I remember him talking about the significant number of casualties he treated. He was very clear that he treated each Allied soldier and each German soldier with the same professional care. That to me was a powerful illustration of showing mercy as he treated with equal care his compatriots and those who had been firing lethal bullets at him.

I recall a refection from Mother Teresa that you never know the full consequences of the ripples you set off through one puddle. One act of kindness can set a tone throughout an organisation. We should never underestimate the consequences of our seeking to be merciful.

Stuart Blanch, a former Archbishop of York, in his reflective book on the Beatitudes, describes this Beatitude as like 'a great rock in a desert sand'. He said it reminds us to be compassionate, concerned, gracious and tender with a self-giving generosity of time and resource. Bringing mercy will be different in different contexts.

I was talking with a prison chaplain recently who reflected on bringing kindness and hope for prisoners locked in their cells for twenty-three hours a day during the Covid-19 epidemic. Her story was a poignant reminder to me about how we can, through our focused engagement with individuals, bring a sense of loving kindness that uplifts and brings a sense of hope and the possibility of new life in the most unhappy and unpromising of circumstances.

Sometimes showing mercy might be engaging with others to encourage them to become the best version of themselves. Sometimes the longer-term demonstration of being merciful is about addressing injustice and seeking to build a kinder culture in the organisations of which we are part.

Sometimes we need to be merciful to ourselves and stop putting too much pressure on ourselves. Stepping aside for a period to be renewed and refreshed is sowing the seeds for our rejuvenation. Being merciful to ourselves is equally as important as being merciful to others. This is not about indulgence or escapism; it is about the harsh reality that if we do not look after our own wellbeing we will not be in a position where we can be merciful to others.

John was not sure whether showing mercy was a sign of strength of weakness. Two of his team were not performing well and both articulated reasons for their frequent absences. John's initial reaction was to be supportive of both of them and not be too demanding. Eventually he discovered that one of the individuals had been moonlighting doing another paid job in parallel. When John confronted the individual, he was very defensive arguing that he needed to have two jobs in order to have enough resource to look after their family.

With the second individual John began to understand more how she responded to stress. She was having mental health challenges and was not able to focus effectively if the stress level went above a certain amount. John felt more sympathy to this individual and arranged for her to have some counselling and to allowed her to work more flexibly, while at the same time John was clear about the expectations this individual would need to keep delivering.

What was tempering John's mercy to these two individuals was that other people in the team were having to work exceptionally hard in order to cover their absences. John was clear to the individual who had been moonlighting that he needed to fulfil his contractual commitments. He set clear expectations with this individual about what he was expected to deliver and his hours of work and was explicit that his performance would be closely monitored. John wondered whether he was treating these two individuals in a differential way that was justified. He felt that he was carefully balancing the needs of both mercy and justice, holding together the interests of both the individuals and the rest of the team.

Idika was conscious that her team had been through a very difficult period. Resources had got tighter. Her clients were getting increasingly grumpy. The team was not able to deliver to the standard they wanted in terms of the service they provided. There was a risk of people getting very edgy with each other and showing frustration within the team when they had to keep cool when engaging with their clients.

Idika organised a three-hour workshop for the team based around the theme of what does it mean to show mercy to each other and to ourselves. This led to a frank, open conversation about what caused people to get frustrated and edgy with each other. They reflected on when people had shown generosity of spirit with each other and brought kindness and mercy.

The dialogue allowed frustration to be described and generous acts of mercy to be talked through. As a result, the team became more comfortable sharing when there was frustration and were more explicit in showing mercy and kindness to each other. As a result, Idika felt the team was nudging in the right direction while recognising that frustrations would inevitably build up from time to time.

For Reflection

- When you observe others demonstrating mercy in the workplace, has it been a sign of strength or weakness?
- How best do you balance bringing mercy and justice when every situation is different?
- What might be the risks of showing too much mercy?
- When can it be too risky to show too much justice?
- What might be the red lines for you, outside which mercy needs to be subjected to justice and decisive action?
- How important to you is showing mercy as a leadership quality?

9

Blessed Are the
Pure in Heart

The full Beatitude is, 'Blessed are the pure in heart, for they will see God'.

In ancient societies purity and cleanliness was essential to ensuring health and wellbeing. Purity was extended to cover words and actions. The Prophet Isaiah described himself as a man of unclean lips. He had a vision of a seraph (a celestial being) who touched his mouth and says, 'see this touch on your lips, your guilt is taken away and your sin atoned for'. Isaiah then senses the voice of God and his call to be a prophet. The essence of the vision of God in the Hebrew tradition is that this often comes to people who are wholly unprepared for it.

Psalm 51 focuses on purity and looking forward with a steadfast spirit with the exhortation to 'Cleanse me with hyssop, and I shall be clean; wash me and I shall be whiter than snow. Hide your face from my sins and blot out all my iniquity. Create in me a pure heart, oh God, and renew a steadfast spirit within me'.

The word 'pure' has a long history in the Greek and Hebrew language. It was associated with the outward cleansing of the body and preoccupations with diet and prohibitions about the eating of unclean animals. The language of unclean was extended to cover other groups of people. A Samaritan woman was considered unclean from childhood and could not be approached by a Jew without a risk of impurity.

Jesus found himself seriously at issue with the Rabbis on this type of issue, with his engagement with the Samaritan woman at the well being a clear infringement of the purity laws related to Samaritans. Jesus broke the taboos and observed purity of heart rather than following precise practices about cleanliness and assumptions about the apparent purity or impurity of different peoples.

Jesus broke the taboos. He made a practice of eating with sinners. He insisted on touching lepers. When speaking to the crowds he emphasized the importance of their understanding that, 'nothing outside you can defile you by going into you, rather it is what comes out of you that defiles you'. Jesus was focusing responsibility on the individual to express purity in their words and actions.

The words pure and heart are central within the New Testament with pure mentioned 28 times and heart over 100 times. There is a focus on bringing an openness of heart whereby the disciples are to proclaim the kingdom of generosity where people who have freely received are invited to then freely give.

Augustine believed that the pure in heart were able to see and understand eternal truths and appreciate the relevance of Christ's approach and teaching in different ways and places. They increasingly recognised the attributes of Jesus in others. We are on a long journey becoming hopefully more pure in heart as we become increasingly perceptive about the inner emotions of those around us.

The Psalmist talks about the importance of an 'undivided heart'. The Apostle James talks of a double-minded person as being inherently unstable, whereas an undivided heart speaks of steadfastness. That resolve and steadiness might need to touch into a number of areas concurrently. Isaiah talks of washing yourselves, making yourselves clean, removing the evil of your doing, learning to do good, seeking justice, rescuing the oppressed, defending the orphan and pleading for the widow.

As we seek to purify our hearts, we are seeking to recognise the biases we carry. What we deny, cannot be healed, while what we acknowledge and openly confess, can open the door to cleansing and reshaping our perspective going forward.

Matthew brings realism that what is in our heart determines what we say and do. He writes in chapter 12; 'For out of the overflow of the heart, the mouth speaks. Good people bring good things out of the good stored in them and evil people bring evil things out of the evil stored up in them'. As a leader being pure in heart involves bringing openness and honesty, and looking at situations without preconceptions or biases. It involves being clear about prejudices or preconditions that shape our approach and being able to set them aside so that people and contexts can be understood in a different way.

Being pure in heart involves looking at our own motives objectively and openly. It involves understanding the inner motives of others and not being taken in by appearances. Expectations or assumptions about people's behaviour can keep reinforcing positive standards of engagement, and help identify where there is a lack of alignment when seeking to work together.

Sometimes we have to deal with issues and prejudices that are hidden at the bottom of our hearts. There may have been painful experiences or dialogues in the past that we have not fully dealt with. We have not entirely forgiven those we felt took advantage of us or treated us unfairly. When we accept that deep-seated pain or resentment is holding us back, we may need to be merciful to ourselves and seek to box or depersonalise past experiences in order to seek to move on.

Purity of heart involves being authentic in the way we are open to others and truthful in our perspectives. Being pure of heart is the consequence of embracing the earlier beatitudes: namely, being aware of our brokenness and limitations, mourning how we have hurt others, being self-aware enough to seek honest feedback, seeking to do right in our words and actions, and being merciful and forgiving to ourselves and others. When we have been through these steps we come into our work with a 'clean heart', freed from the burdens of regret and fear that can limit our creativity and our capacity to engage at our best with our work, our colleagues and those around us.

There are moments when we need to be confronted by our own cold-heartedness when we have not treated people with the generosity and warmth that we might have done. Cold-heartedness may be a defence mechanism when we feel unable to do all that is expected of us.

We may be wary in unknown or unpredictable situations. Such wariness might be interpreted as cold-heartedness when it is our being astutely wary. We may be unsure about someone's motives and whether we can entirely trust them and have to reflect on how we are both warm and wary in such situations. Cold heartedness might protect us from risk, but can also hold us back from building rich partnerships going forward.

What is in our heart determines our mindset in how we approach situations and how we seek to influence others. If we think that a particular endeavour is basically a waste of time, our heart will not be committed to its success. We may pay lip service and engage at the margins without being willing to contribute in any significant way. This is an important warning sign that all is not well. In any team endeavour we will be more committed to some elements than others, but it is worth exploring our reasons and motives when we feel half-hearted about a way forward.

If in our heart we can see the potential for constructive change we are much more likely to bring warmth and engagement that will enable others to develop confidence and effectiveness in a new situation. Asking ourselves what our heart is feeling about a situation gives us valuable insights about what is going on and how we and others are likely to react as that situation evolves.

A challenge of leadership is how do we recognise and nurture those who bring pure hearts, and handle those people whose hearts are compromised and not fully engaged or committed. We are balancing engagement with people that is warm alongside keeping an appropriate distance so that we see the reality of what is happening and can sense the motives of those we are seeking to engage with.

The best antidote to being lukewarm towards others is talking with them about what motivates them to do their best work and how we can help them to be at their best. We want to be, and experienced as being, warm hearted and not cold hearted. We want to keep bringing the best out of people bringing a firm belief in new life and hope, while recognising that people are complex.

Jenny felt some resentment in herself when she was asked to take on the leadership of a group of volunteers. She experienced these volunteers as a mixed ability group who had a tendency to complain and apply themselves with varying degrees of enthusiasm. Jenny did not feel particularly warm-hearted towards them but knew that if she was downbeat or cynical that the overall effort from the volunteers would dissipate.

Jenny knew that she had to want to encourage these volunteers from her heart recognising that they brought a mixed set of motivations. She had to deal with the touch of resentment that was at the bottom of her heart and acknowledge the element of cold-heartedness with which she entered the role. Jenny reminded herself that she needed to see the best in each volunteer and accept what they brought and seek to nurture and grow their gifts rather than criticise their limited capability or contribution. Jenny had to declutter her heart and be open to speaking into the hearts of these volunteers to motivate and inspire them in their shared enterprise.

Jules was not entirely convinced about the role he had just been given within the consultancy. He had reluctantly accepted the role and did not particularly want to listen to his boss or others. There was a blinkeredness which was soon irritating other people. Early on his boss spoke frankly to him about this blinkeredness and challenged him to think about his motives in saying yes to this role.

His boss was clear that Jules needed to shift his mindset into a position where he wanted to do this role and then do it with an open heart without bias or reluctance. This conversation was initially a shock for Jules but then cathartic in prompting Jules to reflect on his motives and bring an uncluttered heart and mind to lead this important project well. What worked had been the combination of the frankness and affirmation that Jules' boss had shown. The result was a new wholeheartedness in the approach taken by Jules. He was more deliberate in listening well to others, especially those who had been critical of him. He was now more accepting of responsibility, was engaging with an open heart and was willing to lean into hard conversations.

For Reflection

- How best do you handle your moments of being lukewarm or cold-hearted?
- What issues at the bottom of your heart can distort the way you engage with new assignments and people?

- What needs to be cleansed or decluttered from past experiences or prejudices to enable you to lead well going forward?
- How best do you ensure you are honest with yourself about your own motives and assess carefully the motives of those you are working with?
- In what ways does your mindset need to be re-shaped to bring openness and purity of thinking and what practical steps might you take to achieve this?

Blessed Are the
Peacemakers

The full text of the Beatitude is 'Blessed are the peace-makers, for they will be called children of God'.

When have you been able to be a peacemaker? Perhaps you have encouraged two people to talk to each other when there has been a disagreement. Perhaps you have enabled individuals to see events from another person's point of view. Sometimes you have tried to be a peace-maker and felt rejected and frustrated. You carry the bruises of peace-making that did not work out as you had hoped. Maybe you want to be a peacemaker but hold back because you do not want to offend.

Was Jesus a peacemaker? You might not have thought so if you were a Pharisee and heard yourself described by Jesus as a hypocrite, a snake and a viper. You might not have thought of Jesus as a peacemaker if you were a stall-holder in the Temple when Jesus overturned your table. You might have heard Jesus say, 'I do not come to bring peace but a sword' when he sought to shock people into thinking into the future in a new way.

The Gospel writer, Luke, sees Jesus in a different light. He starts his Gospel with words about 'our Lord shining on those living in darkness and guiding our feet in the ways of peace'. The message of the Angels at the birth of Christ is that the Messiah brings peace to those of good-will. When Jesus rides into Jerusalem the disciples rejoice saying, 'blessed is the King who comes in the name of the Lord. Peace in heaven and glory in the highest'.

The Gospel writer John describes peace as a personal experience rather than as a desirable social condition. He quotes Jesus saying, 'peace I leave with you: my peace I give you', and 'I have told you these things so that you may have peace'. John describes Jesus standing above the disciples and saying, 'peace be with you'.

Hebrew scriptures echo these two dimensions of peace within ourselves and peace within the community and the nations. Isaiah talks of a God who will keep in perfect peace those whose mind is steadfast. Isaiah also talks about building society where justice and righteousness dwell together with the fruit of righteousness being peace, quietness and confidence. This raises the question of what does being a peacemaker mean in our current culture or society?

This has been described as the civic Beatitude. It is a call to be engaged in the community and the workplace as a peacemaker, potentially encouraging, steering, prompting or nudging. It can be helping people to see the other person's perspective and enabling colleagues to turn resentment into a recognition of why someone behaves in the way they do.

Sometimes seeking to be a peacemaker can involve helping individuals to face up to uncomfortable truths and to recognise their accountabilities. It might mean enabling them to see how they have contributed to discord and how they are expected by those in authority to face up to reality. We are perhaps able to speak truth because we are doing self-reflection ourselves in practising the ways of the Beatitudes. This is at the unpopular end of being a peacemaker. We may not be 'turning over the tables' but we may be suggesting that the table is about to collapse and offering ways forward.

One individual I work with has to contend with members of the public who become quite irate about the decisions he is called upon to make. He periodically receives letters signed, 'yours furiously'. His approach to being a peacemaker is to bring tact and diplomacy in his engagement. He seeks to build rapport with critics about what he is seeking to take forward. He seeks to listen carefully but not be brow-beaten by those who take an opposing view or do not give the same significance to points he is most concerned about.

He is conscious that sometimes the people he is trying to engage with in a peaceful and calm way will be rude to him and seek to manipulate what he is saying. It feels more like trying to keep the peace than peace-making. He recognises that he needs to be clear on his facts and the reasons for the decisions he is implementing, while not being brow-beaten by a deluge of emotive words or pains of emotional blackmail.

When we live our lives with a pure heart we can be calm and confident enough inside so that we make room for the opinions of others and look at their ideas objectively and not defensively. We can bring peace when we acknowledge the intent of others, even if we do not fully agree with their viewpoints. By calmly listening to and engaging with those who differ from us, we can sometimes bring a collective calmness in surprising ways.

Perhaps one application of this Beatitude is to reflect on how best you allow yourself to be at peace with yourself. Often our greatest battles are within ourselves as we contend with disappointment, mixed motives, frustration or a lack of recognition. Making peace with yourself may be about becoming more accepting of who you are and being a shade more comfortable in your own skin.

The Gospel writer John recognised that it is possible to experience concurrently tribulation in the world and peace in the heart. Sometimes we are having to live with this contradiction of facing into aggravation and discord, while seeking to preserve as much peacefulness in our heart as possible.

What might enable us to make peace with ourselves? It might mean letting go of a long-held ambition. It might mean seeking to gradually take off a burden of accountability that is weighing us down. It might mean coming to terms with the current reality of our health, finances or family context. We can feel encouraged that as we make peace with ourselves, we can feel lightened and blessed with a fresh sense of how life can be going forward, bringing a new spring in our step and more hope in our heart. It can involve us becoming more honest with and about ourselves, and becoming more at peace with the gifts we have been given and less frustrated about the gifts we have not been given.

A pertinent question is how do we handle ourselves when our attempts at making peace may fall apart and we feel far from blessed by events beyond our influence or control? We can feel a sense of calling or responsibility to build peace in a particular context, and then feel disappointed when our best intentions are ignored or misrepresented. We fall into the trap of thinking that if our attempts at peace-making are unsuccessful, that we have failed and have let others down. But if the other party is not willing to engage in peace-making, then all our efforts are likely to fail.

My mother tried for years to build a relationship with a close relative who had broken away from the family. My mother felt she carried a burden throughout her later life that she had failed and that the broken relationship was somehow her fault. The truth was that all her noble efforts to rebuild a relationship were not reciprocated. Many of us will have experienced an echo of this where we have put our hearts and soul into seeking to build peace and have felt rejected and even maligned.

Peace-making does not always work. Jesus did not make peace with the Pharisees. His overtures about a new way of living were often rejected. It was not a peaceful crucifixion, and yet, in his pain there was compassion for his mother and words of encouragement for one of those crucified alongside him.

This Beatitude invites us to be peace-makers, to be an influence for good in all walks of life, bringing hope and restoration and drawing out where discord and inappropriate behaviour is undermining the peace for others. Shalom is not the absence of conflict: bringing shalom or peace is about seeking to contribute to finding wholeness where there is mutual understanding and respect.

Helping to build peace in any context will rarely be straightforward. Part of engaging with peace-making is about making peace with ourselves. It involves accepting that we will rarely see the full consequences of where we have sought to enable others to be at peace with themselves and their friends of colleagues. Being a peace-maker is a long game of seeking to change people's attitudes so that relationships become more forward-looking. It can take time for people to want to change and bring a sense of peace and purpose rather than pain and perniciousness. Often we cannot change others' perspectives: But maybe we can create an environment where they feel safe and supported enough to explore the different expectations and pressures in their hearts.

Peace-making is an art that involves careful listening and engagement. Approaches that work depend on the cultural context and the emotions and temperaments of those involved. Being bold as a peace-maker may start with creating a context where people can talk and see issues from the perspective of others. Being a peacemaker can be tiring, painful and initially unrewarding. The first reaction might be that you are meddling. Good peacemakers do not give up. They adapt their approaches and seek to find a way forward that is going to catch the imagination seeking to build on where there are shared hopes and aspirations.

Two dominant themes in corporate life at the moment are equality and diversity, and bulling and harassment. As we address these issues bringing peace is not about pretending the problems don't exist. Being a peacemaker involves being explicit about the issues and ensuring that clear data is available on what the problems are. Key is then addressing those issues in as direct and inclusive a way as possible, recognising there is a fine line between constructive criticism and unreasonable behaviour that is experienced as bullying.

Sonia was reporting into both her Functional Head and to the Finance Director. She was fully aware that these two individuals were often at loggerheads with each other. Sonia recognised that she had the power to damage that working relationship or to seek to improve it. The mischievous in her was inclined to tell one narrative to one person and a modified narrative to the other person in order to show what she was doing in the best possible light. Sonia recognised that in the long run this type of approach would be counterproductive, but she did not want to make an enemy of either of these two people.

Sonia was very deliberate in the facts she shared with them both, sending them copies of the same submission on sensitive, finance issues. She knew there would be disagreement and she wanted that debate to take place on the basis of an accurate set of facts. She sought to influence how the dialogue was constructed in order to get to an outcome that they could both live with. She was not trying to create a cuddly-type of peace, but she did her level best to enable these two individuals to reach an agreement that they could both live with and justify. This was both exhausting and rewarding for Sonia both professionally and personally, recognising that the agreements sometimes felt quite fragile.

Bill used to get inwardly cross with his boss and most of his colleagues. This frustration led to a disdain which leaked out with his colleagues being increasingly wary of him. Bill recognised that he needed to become more at peace with himself and not let his frustration show so much. In order to build the right sort of forward relationships with colleagues, Bill needed to be less edgy and show a calmer sense of purpose and direction. Bill built breaks into his diary where he could have ten minutes peacefulness walking out of the building. He knew he needed to remind himself to calm down and cheer himself up before trying to enter what felt like a difficult conversation.

Bill accepted there were insights from the Beatitudes which helped him feel more at peace with himself. He was more able to recognise his negative attitudes (poor in spirit), to feel remorse for being over judgemental and impatient of others (mourn), humbled enough to see more clearly the perspectives of others (meek), committed to changing his approach for the benefit of others (righteousness), seeking to understand and bring grace to himself and others (merciful), willing to open his heart to others (pure in heart), and then seeking to be at peace with himself and seeking to build constructive harmony going forward (peacemaker).

For Reflection

- What does it mean to be a peacemaker when those around you are full of angst?
- How best do you handle the apparent disdain of others when you are seeking to be a peace-maker?
- How do you handle situations where your attempts at peace-making fall apart and you feel far from blessed by events beyond your control?
- What might allow you to be more at peace with yourself when handling the frustration and unhappiness of others?

11

Blessed Are Those Who Are Persecuted Because of Righteousness

The full wording is, 'Blessed are those who are persecuted because of righteousness, for theirs is the kingdom of heaven'.

The meaning of the Hebrew word for persecuted is normally, though not invariably, translated as pursued or hunted down. It is a measure of the frequency of this experience in the history of Israel that the world persecuted occurs 130 times in the Hebrew Bible. Jeremiah talks of, 'the Lord is with me like a mighty warrior, so my persecutors will stumble and not prevail'. Persecution had bitten into the heart and mind of the Israelites because they had suffered from their devotion to the Law in a society that was largely alienated from their way of thinking.

Jesus spoke into a situation where his hearers would be well versed in the sufferings of their ancestors. As a nation occupied by the Romans at the time when Matthew wrote his Gospel, the people will have felt vulnerable to persecution from an occupying power.

Paul saw persecution as a fact of life. He himself had been a persecutor of the Christians and recognised that he was likely to receive the same treatment. Paul wrote that people needed to go through hardships in order to enter the kingdom of God. He talks of rejoicing in sufferings. Matthew wrote his gospel at the time when persecution was endemic in the situation created by the fall of Jerusalem.

When Matthew recorded this Beatitude he was recognising that his readers were currently being persecuted as there was animosity towards Christians. He reinforces this identification with the people who are being persecuted by following up this Beatitude with the words, 'blessed are you when people insult you, persecute you and falsely say all kinds of evil against you'. Matthew records Jesus' exhortation to those who are being persecuted to 'rejoice and be glad, because great is your reward in heaven, for in the same way they persecuted the Prophets who were before you'.

Dietrich Bonhoeffer wrote that, 'suffering is the badge of true discipleship'. When suffering in prison prior to his execution, Bonhoeffer went as far as saying that suffering was a joy and a token of God's grace. The persecution Bonhoeffer experienced is in an entirely different league to what we are likely to experience. But there are parallels in what enabled him to endure. He did not give up on standing up for justice and peace. He was able to hold firm in his personal beliefs.

The experience of feeling persecuted takes many different forms. It can be the removal of an individual from their work with no apparent reason or for standing up for what is right, or drawing attention to unethical actions by others. It can involve the humiliation of being walked out of a building under false pretences. Persecution can involve bullying behaviour that renders it impossible to continue to work in the same environment. Such manipulative behaviour has in the past often been ignored or tolerated.

The persecuted might be those from a particular racial group, or from a particular social or cultural background, or because they have a particular sexual orientation or are of a certain age or have some physical or mental disabilities or health issues. Persecution can be overt or it can be insidious and covert.

Sometimes people can feel persecuted as a result of their being particularly sensitive about how they are treated. A risk is that some people are unaware that their behaviours can be far more detrimental than they realise. Words spoken either without thought, or intended to tease, are sometimes given a greater significant than intended, which can lead to an innocent comment being interpreted as a major, insensitive rebuff.

Those in exposed leadership positions may well feel persecuted when what they have sought to do is exercise their accountabilities responsibly. A headteacher may have excluded a pupil from a school because of inappropriate behaviour and then be criticised by vocal parents who feel their youngster has been unfairly treated. A hospital senior manager may feel personally attacked when the

Regulator expresses concerns about standards within the hospital. The football manager can feel persecuted by hostile supporters after they have lost a couple of matches in a row. Feeling persecuted is part of the leadership experience of many people, but it is mostly the persecution from words and indignation, rather than a risk to life and limb.

A sense of persecution can bite into our hearts and make us feel bitter and resentful, but a degree of criticism and negative feedback can remind us of where we have made false steps in the past and can strengthen our resolve going forward.

Someone who has lost their job on say three or four occasions has a choice about whether they feel persecuted by unfairness and authority, or whether each experience is shaping who they are and what contribution they might be able to bring as a citizen and as a leader going forward.

Putting persecution into relative proportion is key. We may feel highly aggrieved about the way we have been treated, but that treatment might have been justified or modest compared to the experiences of others. We can become highly indignant in a way which wastes our energy and keeps fuelling resentment and limits our scope to move on in as accepting a way as possible.

In the workplace there are times when we feel hard done by. Perhaps there is gossip about us that is unkind with people saying mean things about us behind our back. We can easily feel indignant and persecuted when what we are experiencing is the trivia of office politics. There is a risk that we see ourselves as being persecuted when others observe office humour that might have got a little out of hand.

Hardship shapes each of us. An element of criticism, negativity or even persecution is inevitable. It is not helpful to be over-sensitive about behaviour or humour which is not the way we would do things. On the other hand, as a leader it is our duty to recognise when individuals in an organisation are being unfairly treated and are at risk of being or feeling undervalued, left out or even persecuted.

Someone in an organisation who has been unfairly treated and continues to show resolve without bearing a grudge can become a wonderful role model. Their persistence becomes admired by others with potentially a profound quiet influence for good on others who are thereby encouraged to show the same resolve in adversity.

Some people have experienced acute or insidious persecution at work. They have been vilified or victimised over a long period. It is far worse than incidental or missplaced criticism. They may be ostracised because of what they have said in the past. Often the individual has nowhere else to go and does not have the financial freedom to resign and move on. They have to stick at their work feeling the burden of harsh eyes upon them. They recognise that they have not always been the perfect colleague but seek with dignity and courtesy to engage and move forward their work in as constructive away as possible.

Farookh was at risk of feeling hard done by. As an auditor he kept pointing out risks and dangers. He developed a reputation of always seeing the negative rather than the positive. People were wary about talking to him as they would feel deflated as a result of a conversation which had resulted in them feeling inadequate. The result was both Farookh and the people he was engaging with felt persecuted. Farookh received sound advice from his boss that he needed to win over people from elsewhere in the organisation. This was not about lowering the standards he was expecting to be attained, but it was about how he expressed his concerns so that he was building much more of a sense of shared endeavour rather than criticism.

Not surprisingly, this change of approach from Farookh led to his clients being more willing to talk to Farookh at an early stage with Farookh feeling appreciated rather than persecuted. His clients fully accepted that Farookh had a 'policing' role but were more willing to work with him at an early stage in seeking to find solutions rather than seeking to pretend that problems did not exist. For both parties, the experience of persecution was avoidable as approaches were developed, which built a greater sense of mutuality.

Emma felt she had been mistreated in her previous role. Her boss had been very demanding of her and given her very little credit. After two years she was exhausted and deflated. The opportunity came to apply for another job which she enjoyed much more and felt liberated within it. Emma could easily have felt that she had been persecuted in her previous role by a boss who she felt was only thinking of their own career.

Emma did not want to bear any resentment because she knew this would eat her up, nor did she want her previous boss's behaviour to continue to affect her successors in a detrimental way. Emma decided to do two things: the first was to have a frank conversation with her previous boss in which she talked honestly about how she had experienced working for him. Emma entered that conversation with a degree of trepidation and was pleasantly surprised that her previous boss was very quiet in the conversation and acknowledged that sometimes his behaviour was not acceptable.

The second step Emma took was to draw a line under that feeling of being persecuted in her previous role. She did not want to carry any bitterness forward. Rather, what she held in her mind was how the previous job had shaped her and developed some valuable thinking and ways of approaching the tasks before her.

Tom recognised that he was about to be blamed for a decision that had not worked out well. Lots of people were involved in contributing to the original decision. Someone had to take the blame and all the indications were that he would be held personally accountable and removed from his current role. How was Tom going to react? He could allow himself to feel a victim and a martyr. He could fight back recognising that he might be bruised and battered with his reputation further tarnished.

Tom recognised that he could be straight and factual in describing what he had done and why, and then seek to move on with his head held up high. Tom did not want to be demeaned by actions from others which bordered on persecution. He had a life outside work that sustained him. He was not going to let himself be defined by those who, to save their own reputations, wanted to place blame on him.

For Reflection

- When and how has a degree of pain in a previous role helped shape and sharpen your leadership?
- When are you at risk of treating a minor rebuff as your being persecuted?
- How do you respond when you observe that others are beginning to experience a degree of unfairness that could rapidly turn into discrimination or even persecution?
- How best do you create an environment which is challenging and enables people to develop, while not impacting on them in a way that they experience as unfair, unreasonable and detrimental?

12

Engaging with Our Internal and External Landscape

The Beatitudes provide a sequence of interconnected lenses through which we can see and engage with our internal and external landscapes in a new way. They provide an antidote to self aggrandisement and at the same time prompt us to be bold and courageous. They both remind us of the poverty of our actions and help us focus on where we can be a constructive influence for good. They enable us to sit with grief and sadness, and then view with humility and an open heart the opportunities before us. They remind us that life involves hungering to make a constructive difference and being rebuffed and sometimes criticised, ostracised or ignored for seeking to do what we believe is the right thing.

The Beatitudes provide a way of engaging with our inner landscape, viewing our hopes, fears and aspirations in a fresh way. They recognise the harsh reality of life that includes times of disappointment, grief, inadequacy, duplicity and pain. They help reframe inner hunger and thirst into a constructive force for good and not just a means of sustaining our physical wellbeing. They remind us how looking to draw out the best in others, bringing purity of motive, and seeking to bring harmony, renews and refreshes our own inner motivations and enables us to move forward with grounded hope and optimism. They remind us that criticism, disdain and harassment may be part of our life experience too.

The Beatitudes provide a way of engaging with our external landscape bringing insights about both reality and purpose. As we move through our weeks and years we see life unfold in unexpected ways. We can then decide which routes to take and make choices about our attitudes and actions. There are mountains in the way some of which are insurmountable. There are rivers which we do not see how to cross. We will need patience to persevere.

As we move through our external landscape the Beatitudes provide a perspective about learning from when we make wrong decisions, or come through grief and disappointments. They help us recognise our need to bring an open mind and to be as clear as we can be about what positive difference we want to make in the situations in which we find ourselves. The Beatitudes provide a framework to balance mercy and justice, to bring purity and openness in our motives, to seek to address discord through building harmony and shared purposes, and to accept that doing and saying what needs to be said will sometimes make us unpopular and resented.

Whatever your personal context I hope that this short book has prompted you to reflect in new ways about the leadership opportunities and challenges before you. I hope that the Beatitudes keep providing you with new insights as you look through the eight interconnected lenses and engage with your internal and external landscapes with hope and expectation.

Selected Bibliography

Barclay, William. *The Plain Man Looks at the Beatitudes.* London: Fontana Books, 1963.

Blanch, Stuart. *Way of Blessedness.* London: Hopper & Stoughton, 1985.

Carter, Warren. *Matthew: Storyteller, Interpreter, Evangelist.* Massachusetts: Hendrickson, 2004.

Fawcett, Nick. *Beatitude Attitudes: Exploring the Blessing of Christian Discipleship.* Minneapolis: Augsburg, 2004.

France, R T. *Matthew: Evangelist and Teacher.* Exeter: Paternoster, 1989.

France, R T. *Matthew: Tyndale New Testament Commentaries.* London: IVP, 1985.

Green, Michael. *The Message of Matthew.* London: IVP, 1988.

Pennington, Jonathan. *The Sermon on the Mount and Human Flourishing.* Grand Rapids: Baker Academic, 2018.

Quercus. *Speeches that Changed the World*. London: Quercus, 2015.

Stott, John. *The Beatitudes: Developing Spiritual Character*. London: IVP, 1988.

Spurgeon, C H. *The Beatitudes*. London: Amazon, 2012.

Stanton, Graham. *A Gospel for a New People: Studies in Matthew*. Edinburgh: T&T Clark, 1992.

Stewart, Steve. *The Beatitudes for a Time of Crisis*. Rio Rancho: Impact Nations, 2020.

Wright, Tom. *Matthew for Everyone: Part 1*. London: SPCK, 2012.

Acknowledgments

The Beatitudes have long been a source of fascination for me. Over recent years I have come to appreciate their significance in a more poignant way when working with senior leaders in a range of different contexts. They are prompts for thought in a wide range of different situations.

During the dark days of lockdown in the early part of 2021 putting together the book has been a good way of looking forwards rather than feeling held back by the limitations of lockdown.

I am very grateful to a number of people who have given me very valuable insights about the Beatitudes. In particular I want to thank Paul Davies, Ruth Sinclair, Marlene Parsons, Ian Kenyon, John Coster, Ruth Ackroyd,. Henrietta Blyth and Simon Taylor who have all given me insightful comments. Some of the material was first used in a couple of talks at the Busbridge and Hambledon Benefice in the Guildford Diocese. It was feedback from those talks which encouraged me to develop the ideas and put them into this short book. I learnt much from the perceptive talks given by Philippa Baker and Gertrud Sollars in the same series.

I am very grateful to Jackie Tookey who has typed the manuscript with her exceptional, calmness, thoroughness and efficiency. Tracy Easthope has been an admirable executive assistant and has enabled me to use my time as effectively as possible so that this book could be written.

I am grateful to Bill Reimer who agreed to take forward this manuscript at Regent College Publishing. Bill has been a great source of practical wisdom at Regent College, Vancouver over many years. Robert Hand has been assiduous in ensuring a clear, final product.

I am grateful to Andrew Baker who has contributed the foreword to the book. Andrew brings the intellectual disciple of a Judicial mind, alongside a compassionate heart and a deep desire to enable people to grow in wisdom and understanding, as exemplified by his extracurricular activity of coaching junior football teams.

I particularly want to acknowledge how much I have enjoyed working with individuals and teams across the world as they address their leadership challenges. It is the wisdom I learn from them that feeds directly into suggestions about how the Beatitudes can inform and enhance the way we lead in the most demanding and unexpected situations.

A particular thanks goes to Frances for her support and encouragement: Frances is always a source of practical common-sense.

Books and Booklets
by Peter Shaw

Mirroring Jesus as Leader. Cambridge: Grove, 2004.

Conversation Matters: How to Engage Effectively with One Another. London: Continuum, 2005.

The Four Vs of Leadership: Vision, Values, Value-Added, And Vitality. Chichester: Capstone, 2006.

Finding Your Future: The Second Time Around. London: Darton, Longman and Todd, 2006.

Business Coaching: Achieving Practical Results Through Effective Engagement. Chichester: Capstone, 2007 (co-authored with Robin Linnecar).

Making Difficult Decisions: How to Be Decisive and Get the Business Done. Chichester: Capstone, 2008.

Deciding Well: A Christian Perspective on Making Decisions as a Leader. Vancouver: Regent College Publishing, 2009.

Raise Your Game: How to Succeed at Work. Chichester: Capstone, 2009.

Effective Christian Leaders in the Global Workplace. Colorado Springs: Authentic/Paternoster, 2010.

Defining Moments: Navigating Through Business and Organisational Life. Basingstoke: Palgrave/Macmillan, 2010.

The Reflective Leader: Standing Still to Move Forward. Norwich: Canterbury, 2011 (co-authored with Alan Smith).

Thriving in Your Work: How to Be Motivated and Do Well in Challenging Times. London: Marshall Cavendish, 2011.

Getting the Balance Right: Leading and Managing Well. London: Marshall Cavendish, 2013.

Leading in Demanding Times. Cambridge: Grove, 2013 (co-authored with Graham Shaw).

The Emerging Leader: Stepping Up in Leadership. Norwich: Canterbury, 2013 (co-authored with Colin Shaw).

100 Great Personal Impact Ideas. London: Marshall Cavendish, 2013.

100 Great Coaching Ideas. London: Marshall Cavendish 2014.

Celebrating Your Senses. Delhi: ISPCK, 2014.

Sustaining Leadership: Renewing Your Strength and Sparkle. Norwich: Canterbury, 2014.

100 Great Team Effectiveness Ideas. London: Marshall Cavendish, 2015.

Wake Up and Dream: Stepping into Your Future. Norwich: Canterbury, 2015.

100 Great Building Success Ideas. London: Marshall Cavendish, 2016.

The Reluctant Leader: Coming Out of the Shadows. Norwich: Canterbury, 2016 (co-authored with Hilary Douglas).

100 Great Leading Well Ideas. London: Marshall Cavendish, 2016.

Living with Never-Ending Expectations. Vancouver: Regent College Publishing, 2017 (co-authored with Graham Shaw).

100 Great Handling Rapid Change Ideas. London: Marshall Cavendish, 2018.

The Mindful Leader: Embodying Christian Principles. Norwich: Canterbury, 2018.

100 Great Leading Through Frustration Ideas. London: Marshall Cavendish, 2019.

Leadership to the Limits: Freedom and Responsibility. Norwich: Canterbury, 2020.

The Power of Leadership Metaphors: 200 Prompts to Stimulate Your Imagination and Creativity. London: Marshall Cavendish, 2021.

Those Blessed Leaders: The Relevance of the Beatitudes to the Way We Lead. Vancouver: Regent College Publishing, 2021.

Forthcoming

Shaping your Future. Norwich: Canterbury, 2022.

Booklets

Riding the Rapids. London: Praesta, 2008 (co-authored with Jane Stephens).

Seizing the Future. London: Praesta, 2010 (co-authored with Robin Hindle-Fisher).

Living Leadership: Finding Equilibrium. London: Praesta, 2011.

The Age of Agility. London: Praesta, 2012 (co-authored with Steve Wigzell).

Knowing the Score: What We Can Learn from Music and Musicians. London: Praesta, 2016 (co-authored with Ken Thompson).

The Resilient Team. London: Praesta, 2017 (co-authored with Hilary Douglas).

Job Sharing: A Model for the Future Workplace. London: Praesta, 2018 (co-authored with Hilary Douglas).

The Four Vs of Leadership: Vision, Values, Value-Added and Vitality. London: Praesta, 2019.

The Resilient Leader. London: Praesta, 2020 (co-authored with Hilary Douglas).

Leading for the Long Term: Creating a Sustainable Future. London: Praesta, 2020 (co-authored with Hilary Douglas).

(Copies of the booklets above can be downloaded from the Praesta website)

About the Author

Peter Shaw has coached individuals, senior teams and groups across six continents. He is a Visiting Professor of Leadership Development at Chester, Newcastle, De Montfort, Huddersfield, and Surrey Universities, and is a Professorial Fellow at St John's College, Durham University. He has been a member of the Visiting Professorial Faculty at Regent College, Vancouver since 2008 and is a Visiting Professor at the Judicial College in Melbourne. He has written thirty books on aspects of leadership; some have been translated into seven different languages.

Peter's first career was in the UK Government where he worked in five Government Departments and held three Director General posts. Peter has been a member of governing bodies in higher and further education. He is a licensed lay minister (Reader) in the Anglican Church and plays an active role in the Church of England at parish, diocesan and national levels. He is a Lay Canon of

Guildford Cathedral and Chair of Guildford Cathedral Council.

Peter holds a doctorate in Leadership Development from Chester University. He was awarded an honorary doctorate at Durham University for 'outstanding service to public life', and an honorary doctorate by Huddersfield University for his contribution to leadership and management.

In his coaching work Peter enables leaders and teams to use their freedoms as leaders to best effect. Peter draws from his wide experience both as a leader and as a coach of leaders in many different contexts. He seeks to bring insights drawn from his experience of leading and coaching, and bring an understanding underpinned by his Christian faith and understanding. His focus is on enabling individuals and teams to step up in their effectiveness so that they have a clear vision about what they are seeking to do, apply the values that are most important to them, know how to bring a distinctive value-added and recognise their sources of vitality.

Peter has completed over forty long-distance walks in the UK, with the Yorkshire Dales being his most favoured area for walking. Seven grandchildren help him belie the fact that he was born in the first half of the twentieth century.

Lightning Source UK Ltd.
Milton Keynes UK
UKHW012127070122
396788UK00002B/198